Th ... Obstacles

Celebrating the Silver Lining in Difficult Days

Kathryn Johnson

Kathryn

ISBN: 9781720137993

Imprint: Independently published

Publisher: Kathryn Johnson

Editor: Nina Shoroplova

To my parents

with love and gratitude

Contents

Introduction

"Joy is what happens to us
when we allow ourselves to recognize
how good things really are."
—Marianne Williamson

There are very few guarantees in life. One thing is for sure. Everyone will, at some point, encounter obstacles or challenges. Another thing that is true of practically everyone is they want to be successful. It has been found that the number one factor of success is attitude. Positive people tend to be much more successful under the same circumstances than those with a poor attitude. It has also been found that happiness is desired more than success.

Furthermore, you will undoubtedly experience times when despite your best efforts you do not reach your goal. Often when you have many obstacles in your life, you are likely to breed more obstacles. Then how do you go through life and be happy when obstacles are a given and you have no guarantee of success? This book will teach you how.

In each chapter, I share with you my life experiences with obstacles, and what I see as the gifts inside them. Each chapter concludes with a summary and a series of exercises. The exercises provide an opportunity for you to examine where you currently are and to shift to where you want to be. Their purpose is to help you celebrate the silver lining in your life more easily.

We are living in an age when the Internet, social media, and other technologies are connecting us more intimately than ever before. Our communities are becoming much more global. Not only can we now have conversations with people anywhere in the world in an instant, we now have the technology to see them at the same time. Five billion people, or two thirds of the world's population, now carry cell phones that enable them to access information from anywhere in the world in seconds. Increased efficiency in transportation and logistics now makes global trade easier, faster, and in some ways a necessity.

This increased connectivity also comes with drawbacks. Just as we are positively affected by the convenience associated with changes in the way we do things, we can be adversely affected by other people's actions. When someone halfway around the world drops a plastic ring, it flows through to our ocean. It affects the marine life and the economies that rely on it. We all feel it.

It is our responsibility to look after ourselves and handle life's challenges appropriately and to the best of our ability. I also believe we have a social responsibility to our global community. No one exists in a vacuum. What we do affects others. Therefore, it is our responsibility to do the best we can in life not only for ourselves, but for those around us.

Through leading by example and by being the best version of ourselves we know how to be, we raise others up. If we all do our best to raise ourselves and each other up, the world will be better for everyone in the long run.

This book was inspired by the television show *American Ninja Warrior*. The competitors are from all walks of life and have one thing in common: they view obstacles on the course as a metaphor for the challenges in their life. They embrace the obstacles and face them with a hunger that is contagious. The American Ninja Warrior community is incredibly supportive and encouraging of each other. I share the competitors' passion for life and believe that support from others is a major factor in conquering obstacles

I have much joy in my life. I have a loving family, beautiful friends, and a comfortable home. I am enjoying a successful career as a professional accountant. I have an honors business diploma and a bachelor's degree in Psychology. I've competed internationally and won medals for Team Canada. I have won numerous scholarships and awards. I have much gratitude for all my accomplishments and everything I have experienced. For everything—including adversity.

I was born with a physical disability called cerebral palsy. I don't have good days and bad days. It is simply part of my body. Thankfully, my general health is excellent and there is nothing painful or degenerative about my circumstance. It is simply something I must deal with every day. All day.

Since day one, cerebral palsy has affected my mobility, my experience, and my relationships. Most significantly, however, it has impacted my perspective of life and the world in which we live. What some may view as an unfortunate circumstance, I have come to believe is my greatest gift.

Chapter 1 – Why Me?

"Obstacles are not a hindrance
to your spiritual path,
the obstacle is your spiritual path."
—John Newton

One day something very unexpected happened—at 11:24 a.m., I was born.

My delivery into the world was described as instantaneous. I heard later that I was in distress and a forceps delivery was necessary. From my first breath, I demonstrated tenacity and came into the world kicking and screaming at just under four pounds. I was nine weeks premature.

While I was still in the hospital, it was discovered my liver was underdeveloped and not cleaning my blood properly. To correct the concern, I was given a blood exchange. That is just as it sounds. My original blood was removed and simultaneously replaced with new blood.

Thankfully, the procedure was a success with no further complications. I would remain in the hospital for the next few weeks. My home would be an incubator. My time there was spent growing and doing what most babies do in utero. When I grew to five pounds I was able to go home to my family.

When people are faced with obstacles they often ask, "Why me?" I say, "Why not me?"

No one is exempt from challenges in life. No one. Obstacles are not something we experience because someone doesn't like us or because we are being punished. The Universe did not run out of *easy passes* when handing out life paths. Obstacles are simply part of life. They exist for learning and growth. Obstacles provide an opportunity to experience things we otherwise wouldn't. They help us appreciate the areas of life that are working as we would like.

If the forecast was always sunny and it never rained, would we appreciate the sunshine? If we didn't have rain, we would not experience rainbows, or budding trees, or beautiful flowers. Our lakes and rivers would be dry and the fish would have no home. We would never know the fun of splashing in puddles or experiencing the wonder of thunder storms.

It has been my experience, time and time again, that obstacles are a wrapping for our greatest treasures. They hold the wisdom of our greatest teachings, and yes, even the wonder of our greatest joys. It simply depends how we choose to look at them.

Celebrate the Silver Lining

Welcome to your first opportunity to reflect and to celebrate the silver lining. You now have a chance to integrate the principles in this chapter by reflecting on your own experience. In this and each chapter that follows, before you begin, sit in a quiet space. Also make sure you have paper and a pen handy. You may even want to use your favorite journal (visit inspiredbykathryn.com for a free downloadable journal available in fillable and printable format). Feel free to note any insights you have as you move through the exercises below.

Following are some key treasures.

1. No one is exempt from obstacles. They are simply part of life.

2. Obstacles exist for learning and growth and to help you appreciate what you have.

3. Obstacles can be seen as our greatest gifts. It depends on what we choose to focus on.

Keep these points in mind as you move through to the exercises.

1. Make a list of people you know personally or know of who have been successful beyond expectation. How many of those people do you feel have encountered a challenge or what appears to be a disadvantage? How many of those people do you believe are happy? Did you put yourself on the list? Why or why not?

2. What was the last obstacle or challenge you encountered? How

stressful was it for you? What did you learn from it?

3. What do you appreciate more now because of your experience with that last obstacle or challenge? When you think of what you learned and what you now have, do you have greater appreciation for it? Does the situation seem as stressful?

Chapter 2 – What Do I Do Now?

"If you are not part of the solution
you are part of the problem."
—Eldridge Cleaver

Cerebral Palsy. Before my first birthday, that was what the doctors determined was my diagnosis. It is a neuro-muscular condition that is caused by a lack of oxygen to the brain before, during, or shortly after birth. Cerebral palsy (also known as CP) is not degenerative; however, there is no cure. The best course of action is to help the brain improve function by retraining the body. No two cases of cerebral palsy are exactly alike. The brain and the body are complex. The areas affected and the amount of damage can vary significantly.

My parents noticed I wasn't crawling like other babies. I would move my arms and wouldn't bend my legs. Even before I was a year old, it was apparent that the main effects of my CP would be seen in balance, walking, and coordination. For me, this meant starting an intensive therapy program. In theory, the program would help stimulate and retrain my brain.

Therapy sessions were seven days a week, several times a day. Family, friends, and neighbors came to my home to help me. They would help me with stretching, patterning movements that resembled crawling, and playing games with me to help with my eye-hand coordination. I don't remember much of the program except that I had nice people around me and it was mostly fun. I continued with the program for about a year. After that, I started physical therapy at the Rehab Hospital for Children located in Winnipeg.

When I started school at five, I continued with physical therapy at school and at the rehab hospital on my days off. When other kids would be playing outside, I would be with physical therapists. They would help me with stretching, balancing, and learning to manipulate my body in the way that others could do naturally. My physical therapy continued until I was in grade six.

During this time, I also underwent several elective orthopedic surgeries to improve my balance and my walking. The surgeries served to help my body compensate for what my muscles could not do on their own.

I remember therapy being hard work. Sometimes, it was painful and required much concentration. I remember the physical therapists helping me move. My movements at times seemed so minute and yet they were always met with encouragement and praise. Therapy lead me to experience many milestones. I began walking with a walker with wheels, then moved to one that I would lift as I walked. At the age of eight, I began to use elbow crutches with cuffs on the arms. Then at twelve, I began to use two walking canes for walking support.

Surgeries and hospital stays involved many ups and downs. After each surgery, I would usually spend six to eight weeks in a cast with limited mobility. Surgery was often scheduled during school breaks to limit the days I missed at school. Adjusting to my new mobility after the cast was removed was awkward and often painful. Each time I would recover and come to know more mobility than before. For each of my surgeries, I had quality physicians and quality follow-up care. I remember the hospital staff were always supportive and caring.

Today, surgeries are no longer necessary. I also no longer meet with physical therapists. I use two walking canes most of the time. I am able to walk with only one cane as well. I often walk unaided indoors. I find it easier to move around this way as it allows me full use of my hands that are otherwise full with my walking canes. I do my best to remain active and walk as much as possible. It is the best way for my body to remain healthy, strong, and flexible.

Looking back on these times, I know they were responsible for helping shape my perseverance, focus, and stamina. They helped me celebrate small victories and raise the bar for bigger ones. As life has unfolded, I have been called to strengthen these qualities, time and time again.

In any given situation, you cannot control what has already happened. You can, however, control how you choose to respond to what has happened. The key is to maintain a healthy attitude There is no point in hanging on to regrets of the past. It is over. Done. Finished. All you have is the moment of now from which you can move forward. Take time to pause, assess the situation, and learn from it. Move forward with the next most appropriate action. The faster you move forward, with right action in mind, the easier your path becomes.

How quickly you move forward can depend on the situation. Sometimes, in traffic for example, you must change course right away to avoid a mishap. Other times, like working on special projects, you have days or weeks to assess and make changes to your plans. Sometimes, it may be appropriate to take months to pause and reflect on life around you. People may wish to take vacations or sabbaticals and focus inward for a period of time. How much time you take in a given situation will depend on you as an individual and the learning and growth that is required. For any given situation, some people take longer than others to move through to the next step.

To maintain a balanced and joyful life, it is important to recognize when it is time to move forward. It is very common for people to stay stuck in the past due to fear, regret, or uncertainty of how to move forward correctly.

To become aware of these times, there are several things you can do. First, simply become aware of how many days you have been sitting with the situation. If more time has passed than you expected and you still haven't found a solution, then it is likely time to move forward. For example, did you expect to clean up the garage in a month and now all summer has passed? Have you been thinking of moving residences and realized that five years has gone by since you had the original idea?

Another technique you can use is to become aware of your thoughts or of the sensations in your body. If the situation keeps playing over and over in your mind, or you have difficulty sleeping, or you have aches and pains in your body, perhaps it is time to do something different. It is likely a signal that it is time to resolve the past and move forward.

Life is built on relationships. Nothing is accomplished by the efforts of one person alone. We all have a part to play in this world. For example, for breakfast this morning, you may think you accomplished it all by yourself. In reality, it took many. The farmers grew the food. There were workers who transported the food to the store. There were also the personnel who stocked the shelves and bagged your groceries, just to name a few. There were many others behind the scenes who brought the food to your table for breakfast this morning.

To experience joy in life, it is of prime importance to surround yourself with people who can support you. This is true in all aspects of life and it is especially true in difficult situations. For the fact that we are finding something challenging means there is something within us that has yet to be developed. As it is not yet developed in us, we need the support of others to help us to move forward.

Celebrate the Silver Lining

As you work through the exercises below, consider these key treasures.

1. Perseverance, focus, and stamina can carry you a long way toward success. Celebrate small victories. This sets the stage for you to raise the bar for future opportunities.

2. Move forward with the next right action in appropriate timing. The timing varies for each person and the situation.

3. Enlisting the support of others can have tremendous benefits. Others often have different skills or experiences that you can benefit from. As well, their emotional support can be of great service to help you through difficult times.

Here are some questions to help you apply the keys to your own life. Remember to get your paper and pen.

1. What did you expect to have completed by now? Make a list of these tasks. Beside each task, write down something you can do in the next day or two to move toward that goal. If appropriate, you may want to make a timeline to help keep you focused.

2. Why have you not completed these tasks? What in you needs to be developed? What resources are available to you to help you move forward? Can you do some research or call a friend or family member to help you with what you need?

3. Celebrating your progress gives you momentum. As you go about your day take note of your accomplishments. Also pause and be grateful for the positive things, or wins, that you experienced that day. No win is too small to celebrate. It may be something as simple as receiving a phone call from a friend. Continue this practice for at least one week. What do you notice?

Chapter 3 – How Can I Tie This Together?

"Great things are not done by impulse, but by a series of small things brought together."

—Vincent Van Gogh

I was excited! Finally at the age of five, I was starting kindergarten like the other kids. Thankfully, it quickly became apparent I was quite smart. ABCs ... check; count to 100 ... check; colors and shapes ... check. I quickly learned, however, that although I was like other kids on the inside, certain physical things didn't come easily to me. My goal was to be just like everybody else no matter what.

Just like the other kids in kindergarten, I was learning to tie my shoelaces. It seemed to take forever. I remember sitting on the living room floor at my father's feet as he read the newspaper. My shoe with its untied laces was set in front of me.

I was determined to master my task.

Let's see. First cross the laces. Then flip the top lace over and back under the other one to make a knot. That was relatively easy. Then later, I learned to make a loop with one hand and wrap the other lace around the loop. That took a little while, but I mastered it with time.

The toughest part for me was the last step. To reach my goal and tie my shoe, I had to somehow continue to insert the other lace under the part of it I had wrapped around the loop and pull it under and then through to secure my shoe. Victory seemed elusive. I remember wondering if I would ever get it.

As my mother watched my struggle and my frustration build, she realized the difficulty stemmed from the fact I had limited flexibility in my wrist. I was unable to move it freely. Coordination was also a challenge. To tie my shoes, I had to coordinate moving my wrist and pushing the loop through with my other hand. Using both hands at the same time was difficult. This of course was compounded by the fact I was five and the laces seemed so big and awkward in my tiny hands.

My mother helped me with a new strategy. Her idea was to practice turning my wrist in a movement that mimicked what was needed to tie my shoe. I was able to do this relatively quickly without the added complication of the laces to get in the way. Once I was able to do that, learning the task of tying my shoelaces became much easier.

Then one day, after what seemed like hours upon hours of endless practice, practice, and more practice, I was able to knot my laces. I could make the loop; and then wrap the other lace around that loop; and last but not least, I could finally pull that second lace through its wraparound, make the final knot, and tie my shoe. Victory at last!

By this time, I was the last kid in my class to learn how to tie her shoelaces. The important thing was I was still in kindergarten and I did it! Now, I was just like them. I was indeed just like everybody else.

Almost from my first breath, I was presented with obstacles. Whether it was the intensive therapy program I was enrolled in as a toddler; the many hours of therapy in grade school; or learning to tie my shoelaces, I was being taught a very important lesson in problem-solving: break things down into steps. Focus on one thing at a time. Keep at it and you will eventually succeed. This is one of the most important lessons I've ever learned. Be patient with yourself. Divide tasks into manageable concepts. Take them one at a time and eventually things will come together.

If your current strategy doesn't seem to be working, here are some things you can do. Consider a pause. A rest or a change of pace can clear your head, give you a new perspective, and a renewed sense of dedication. It's been my experience that I often get further faster and with greater quality and ease if I remember to take breaks along the way. Remember the great City of Rome was not built in a day. Also remember the expertise and experience of those around you. Everyone has unique life experiences and they just might have the answer you are looking for.

If you give up and take yourself out of the game, there's no way of knowing what your full potential could have been. You will never know where it would have led. You won't learn who you would have met or how you could have impacted the world.

This simple lesson that I learned in kindergarten has been something I have used repeatedly when faced with a new task. Whether it be a school project, planning a vacation, or moving to my first home, the key to every task is to take manageable action steps and keep moving forward. As long as you keep moving forward, you will eventually arrive at your destination.

We are all connected. Looking to the experiences of others can ease your path to success and build your connection. You will experience greater joy, and others will be lifted up by your success as well.

Celebrate the Silver Lining

Following is a review of some keys in the chapter.

1. Divide tasks into manageable concepts. Take them one step at a time. Keep at it. If you take yourself out of the game, you will never know what could have been.

2. If your current strategy is not working, consider pausing to clear your head or gain a new perspective.

3. Consider the unique experiences of others. They can help provide the solution you need, ease your way, and create new connections.

Consider the keys mentioned when moving through the exercises below.

1. Note a task right now that you are struggling with. How can it best be divided up to isolate the part you are struggling with?

2. Have you considered a new strategy or a different perspective?

3. Can you look to an example of someone who has successfully completed the task as a reference or for advice?

Chapter 4 – Why Doesn't This Add Up?

"Failure is simply the opportunity to begin again, this time more intelligently."

—Henry Ford

From a very young age, I demonstrated an obvious aptitude for numbers. I come from a family with several accountants and number crunchers. I loved playing Monopoly with all its different colors of money. As I mentioned earlier, gratefully, I am quite intelligent. I have a great memory. Basic mathematical skills like adding, subtracting, multiplying, and dividing came easily to me. In fact, I remember hardly ever opening a math textbook to study until the ninth grade. I would maintain an A average by doing my weekly assignments alone.

In ninth grade, something changed. Mathematical concepts were now linked to geometry. This was more difficult for me to grasp, and I began to put more hours into my math homework. My grades were reduced to average. What was once a cakewalk now required a considerable amount of effort.

The next year, in grade ten, things became even harder. I received my first D. I was shocked, embarrassed, and frustrated. I was generally a good student and I was doing well in the rest of my classes with average effort. I remember thinking, "Oh well, at least I passed. Maybe next year I will be better."

I wanted to do better. So I studied really hard. I did extra assignments and spent extra time with the teacher for tutoring.

The following year, I struggled with grade 11 math. I wanted to study accounting so I was taking university entrance math courses. I studied as much as I could and final exams came. Weeks later, I received my grade. I had 49 percent. I had failed. As simple as that.

At this point, I had experience with a wide assortment of struggles and challenges in my life. I had never failed a class. I struggled to accept this failure. It was especially difficult since I was so close to passing. At one percent away from a pass, I literally couldn't get any closer to passing and still not make it. It was very frustrating.

I was absolutely determined to graduate with my class the next year in grade 12. So that meant taking this painfully difficult subject that I used to love over again. I did so in summer school. It wasn't my idea of a fun vacation, but it's what I needed to do to reach my goal and graduate with university entrance level math alongside my peers.

It felt strange to walk into a neighborhood school in July when so many others were outside having fun. The school had air conditioning, which was a great comfort. The number of students in the class was much smaller than during the regular term. The teacher was patient and everyone had the time they needed to ask questions.

As I reviewed the material that had given me so much trouble yet again, something interesting began to happen. It began to make sense. Perfect sense. Things that had been so difficult were now coming together. It was as if a fog had lifted. I felt accomplished as one by one I mastered the concepts. I let go of my embarrassment around my failure and realized there were several others who struggled just like I did. What's more, I'm quite sure some of them got less than 49 percent the first time. I completed summer school with an A. I had a renewed sense of confidence in myself.

The lesson for me was just because I had failed to reach my goal on a certain day didn't mean I should give up what I wanted. Sometimes you simply need a different way to look at it. Take a break and come at it from a different angle. With time and a fresh outlook, you may be pleasantly surprised how things start to come together differently.

My challenges with math had caused me to rethink my senior year course selections as well as my future profession. After my subpar grade in university entrance math, I chose to take basic math by correspondence. I found the correspondence math course quite easy. In September, I received my report card with a grade of a B+. By this time I also knew that I had passed the university entrance math. I felt switching paths to the basic math was somehow selling myself short. I didn't want to limit myself. Despite having put in the extra work for basic math correspondence, and knowing that there was likely a hard road ahead of me, I enrolled in university entrance math my senior year of high school. I was determined to pass no matter what.

My teachers advised me to have a backup plan. I would be enrolled in university entrance math for the first semester. That way if I didn't pass the first time, I would have another semester and a second chance to make the grade while still being able to graduate with my peers.

Senior year university entrance math proved to be just as difficult as anticipated. Once again I struggled through long hours of studying and extra time with the teacher after hours. With the end of semester came report cards. Once again I looked at my grade with anticipation. I had received yet another 49 percent.

This was very frustrating. This was my senior year in high school. I had one more chance to enroll in university entrance math or I could take the easy route with the basic math. I wanted to keep my options open. So I chose to continue in university entrance math and once again embark on the hard road of making the grade.

By this time all the extra work was wearing on me. I was in the final semester of my final year of high school. I still struggled despite extra time and attention. Exam time came and then report cards and, thankfully, I received a grade of C. I had passed. I was average. I was on schedule to graduate with my classmates. I was even given an award on graduation day for my efforts.

It took a few chances and a great deal of effort. I changed courses along the way. I kept at it. I gave myself a safety net and a plan B. Eventually, with my commitment and the support and encouragement of others, I made it.

Looking back on this today, I see it as an example of what can be accomplished when you are willing to step outside your comfort zone. It demonstrates what can happen when you are willing to risk failure for the possibility of a victory that is larger than what most people thought you could achieve You may even serve to be an inspiration to others.

Celebrate the Silver Lining

Following are some keys mentioned in the chapter.

1. Failure is not always a sign to give up on your goal. If your goal remains important to you, then persevere.

2. Success is never guaranteed; therefore, have a safety net and/or a plan B. The greater the risk associated with the failure, the more important it is to have a backup plan.

3. Stepping outside your comfort zone and risking failure can be a catalyst to accomplishing more

than anyone ever thought possible.

Following are some questions to help you apply the concepts in the chapter to your own life.

1. Make note of a time when you didn't achieve a goal.

2. If you could do it over again, what would you do differently?

3. Think of a time when you persevered and succeeded. How did you feel?

4. Is there anything you wish you would have done differently?

Chapter 5 – Why Am I Going in Circles?

"There is no passion to be found playing small,
in settling for a life that is less than the one
you are capable of living"
—*Nelson Mandela*

Many of us are inspired by the Olympics. I am no exception. I remember watching track and field at the age of seven and being struck by the ease, speed, and perfection with which the athletes moved their bodies. I was impressed by their athleticism, their strength of character, and their motivation to keep going regardless of the situation.

That was it: I wanted to be an Olympian.

There was something about being the best I could be that appealed to me. The continual striving to improve, doing something solely for the challenge it presented, and the self-satisfaction of succeeding, all in the pursuit of excellence, were profoundly appealing to me.

At the age of eleven, I started a recreational sports program for kids with disabilities. At twelve, I was introduced to track and field. Adaptive sports were relatively new at the time.

Finally, I had found a way to compete. I would use a custom-fitted aerodynamic racing wheelchair and I would compete against those with similar mobility. I could strive for excellence like my able-bodied counterparts I watched in the Olympics.

At thirteen, I went to my first track meet out-of-province. I quickly discovered a whole new world. I met people from all walks of life with a wide range of disabilities. We often shared with each other what it was like to live with a disability, all of us competing in a sport we loved. We shared a passion for competition and a camaraderie that I had never experienced before.

I discovered there is a wide array of different circumstances one can be faced with in the realm of disability. More importantly, I found a new level of understanding and support with my athletic peers through our common experience. I especially learned that the ability to take an honest look at myself and reflect on it with well-intentioned humor and laughter can do wonders for the heart and soul. I had a new level of acceptance and appreciation for who I am and what I can achieve.

I remember being around my peers at school and seeing brilliantly colored team jackets and jerseys. I so badly wanted a uniform of my own and I knew I couldn't participate fairly in their sports. Now I finally felt I had a place in the world. I was given a uniform and equipment. I would attend weekly sports practices, just like my schoolmates. I too had somewhere to be after class.

Throughout high school and university, I was training three times a week and traveling three to four times a year. I juggled all of this with high school and university courses, family time, and social activities. At the age of sixteen, I began to serve on the board of directors for my sports association and on several related committees. One year, I even had the honor of being chosen by my peers to be an athletes' representative for a national sports association.

I had found a place where I could compete at a new level and succeed. I was being recognized by my peers. I was thriving!

At the age of eighteen, I traveled to England for my first international competition. By this time I had been competing nationally for five years.

This was different though; this was the big time. People I would usually compete against were now on the same team as me. We all had the same jacket, Team Canada. I brought home a gold medal and two silver medals from England.

The gold medal I won was in the 800 meter event. The unusual thing about winning that gold medal was I placed dead last by a significant margin. The other competitors were disqualified because they had changed lanes too early. Before the race began, we were shown where we could cut down to the first lane. I remember thinking it looked further along than what I was used to but, when in Rome (or England), do as the Romans. My coach had trained me never to cut in too early. I followed her advice and it definitely paid off. Thanks, Coach.

Receiving medals in England meant I qualified for the World Athletics Championships for the Physically Disabled to be held the following year in Berlin, Germany. This was huge. I had made it! The team had a national trainer and a sports medicine specialist traveling with us. Media—including Canada's TSN (The Sports Network)—also had a presence there.

By this time I had been training for seven years.

When I went to Germany, to my surprise, I was racing with some of the same people that I had raced against at regional meets. There were two women from the United States, one from England, and one from Ireland. I placed third behind the two Americans and proudly took home two bronze medals for the 100 meter and 200 meter events.

I had finally made it to the big leagues. Yet I realized, I had lost my spark. I asked myself, "Why have I traveled halfway around the world to go around in circles with virtually the same competition I've had for years?"

There were very few fans in the stands and the media coverage was sparse compared to what my able-bodied counterparts would receive. I wondered what difference I was making in the world. By this time I had won over 100 medals in various competitions. I was training six days a week while studying at university. My gruelling training schedule and the competition didn't seem to be accomplishing anything for me or anyone else.

At the end of the World Athletics Championships track meet, I decided to retire from racing. I was two years short of the next Paralympic Games. Being an Olympian didn't seem to matter to me anymore. I didn't feel the need to prove anything. I realized that no matter how well I raced, I would never be happy. Technically, I could always go faster. I would never be finished. My training required me to make many personal and physical sacrifices. Life was taking me in a new direction and I didn't want to pay the price anymore.

I look back on this time in my life with great pride and joy. I developed a greater understanding and acceptance of myself by sharing with those of common experience. I was given many unique honors and opportunities. I came to understand a wider view of what the world has to offer. It was a time of great accomplishments. I pushed myself further than I ever thought I would.

I'll be honest; I often wonder what would have happened if I had kept racing. Would I have made the Olympics? Would I have won Olympic medals or records? How long would I have kept racing?

I was twenty-one when I decided to stop. I felt it was the right decision for me at the time to leave my sport. Yet, my body was not yet mature athletically. I had not yet reached my potential. In fact, I was just getting to the point where I could really be outstanding.

There is a fire in me that still burns today. I feel something is unfinished. I hold a strong desire to be exceptional, not for the accolades or the awards, but because exceeding at something demonstrates strength of character and human spirit.

It's quite possible that the reason I still have this fire is because I have not yet experienced my greatest achievement. I will keep doing the best I can at everything I do. You just never know where these efforts will lead me or who they will impact. You never know when a seed will be planted that will not only become a magnificent oak tree but will be a seed responsible for many oak trees to come.

Celebrate the Silver Lining

As you work through the exercises below consider these key treasures:

1. Building a support network of those with experiences similar to yours can be uniquely helpful.

2. Well-intentioned humor can lead to profound acceptance and understanding.

3. Facing challenges can lead to unique life experiences. It can provide opportunities to experience new and exciting events as well as connect with people in different ways.

4. Do what feels right for you. If your original goal no longer holds your desire, give yourself permission to move on. It is possible that moving in a new direction will lead you to something even greater.

Take note of what comes to you as you consider the following in your own life.

1. Consider something you are struggling with at the moment. Do you know someone who is experiencing or has experienced

something similar? Have you considered reaching out to them for support? Are there other methods of support you could consider?

2. Make a list of some challenges you have faced. Despite the discomfort, how many of them have led you to new and positive experiences that you would not have otherwise enjoyed? Make note of what the experiences were and remember how good you felt as a result.

3. Remember any time when you chose to move on from your original goal. When making your choice, did it feel right for you at the time? If it felt right, has it led to something more fulfilling?

Chapter 6 – What Do I Want to Be When I Grow Up?

"The capacity to learn is a gift.
The ability to learn is a skill.
The willingness to learn is a choice."
—Brian Herbert.

From the time I was five, I wanted to be an accountant. My dad is a retired accountant. I remember sorting my Smarties (like M&Ms) on the coffee table when I was a preschooler. First, I would sort them by color and then line them up to see how many of each color there were.

Dad would ask me what I thought would happen if I moved them around. If they were arranged horizontally would there be the same number as if they were arranged vertically?

I quickly figured out that, yes, of course, there was the same number. And then we would eat one or two and see how things had changed.

I've always loved sorting things.

Most of all, I remember watching my dad prepare income tax returns. I loved the whir of the adding machine and the special sound it makes every time a function key is pressed. I was mesmerized by the reams of paper generated by the machine. I was sure I wanted to be an accountant.

As I've mentioned, math came easily to me until I reached high school. With my difficulty in math, I decided to rethink my career path. I wanted to help people and I liked administrative work, so I thought I would study social work. The first step to being a social worker was to take one year of university courses.

I enrolled in the Faculty of Arts at the University of Manitoba. I declared my major in Psychology and my minor in Sociology. My other courses included Economics, French, and Philosophy. I spent countless hours attending classes, reading volumes of text, writing papers, and completing assignments. Remember, I did all this while still training for track, three to six times a week.

After my first year of university, I applied to the Faculty of Social Work at the University of Manitoba. My application was declined. This was disappointing. It was a small faculty. Enrollment was limited to those with above-average grades and other combinations of qualifications. Enrollment was very competitive.

My declined application led me to start the second year of my Arts Degree. I decided to broaden my options. I thought it would be interesting and adventurous to live in another part of Canada. That year, I applied to the School of Social Work at the University of British Columbia, the University of Calgary in Alberta, and Dalhousie University in Halifax.

Despite my best efforts, every one of my applications was declined. With that, I decided it was time to rethink my career path yet again. It looked like social work wasn't meant for me.

As I was unclear what I wanted to pursue as a career, I didn't see any point in spending energy on courses. Realizing I had spent three quarters of my life in school, I decided to take a year off from studies and re-evaluate.

During this time, I also traveled to Vancouver, British Columbia to train one-on-one with the national team coach. I was in Vancouver for three months. I made arrangements to stay with a friend. I didn't have a job and I had only a few thousand dollars saved as I had worked very little while I was in school. I very much enjoyed my time in Vancouver. As I explored the city, I quickly came to understand it had a very different vibe from my home in Winnipeg.

I loved Vancouver. I enjoyed the busyness of the city. The public transportation was much more convenient than I was accustomed to. The weather was amazing. It delivered moderate temperatures, mild winds, and very few insects to spoil the party. Most of all, I loved being surrounded by greenery, the beautiful mountains, and the rhythm of the ocean. I loved the freedom I had to explore.

It felt so strange to not be burdened with studies or employment. The freedom was just what I needed. I also greatly appreciated the time to train with the national coach. We pushed hard and also had many laughs. It was the trip of a lifetime.

I returned to Winnipeg that December. I was still no more certain about what I was going to do for a career.

I decided to complete the final year of my Arts Degree. I did career counseling including aptitude tests. I also began to do research at the university's career center. What was revealed to me as a good match was a career in records management. When I spoke with the career counselor about this option, she cautioned me. She felt my choice might leave me feeling under-challenged.

I also knew that I was a poor typist. A career with intensive data entry was not a good option for me.

With that new understanding, I was drawn to a career in business administration. It was a good general career with many options, a steady demand forecasted for the future, and a decent pay rate. The following January, I embarked on my second course of study, a diploma in business administration. My major would be, what else, but accounting. I had come full circle. I was thankful for my university entrance math courses.

I would definitely be able to put the knowledge I had from my arts degree to good use as I could transfer several courses directly to the Business Administration Program at Red River College in Winnipeg. I didn't submit my application in time for the September enrollment; I was instead eligible to start one semester later in January.

I found community college to be a very different world than the massive classes at the University of Manitoba. Class size at the college resembled those in high school. Instruction was much more personal. I loved the college's straightforward approach of teaching.

Examples were practical and the discussions were relative to current trends.

I was older than many of the students in my class. Given that I could transfer several courses from my previous studies, my course load was lighter than most students'. I was also no longer competing in track. This meant I had a fair amount of extra time on my hands. I was able to focus more time and attention on my assignments.

It was obvious from the start—my academic performance would be above average. The other students in class were quick to notice. I remember two or three times even getting a perfect score on a test. I made the honor roll.

The other students were noticing me because I was excelling at something. This was the first time I felt able-bodied peers noticing me for my strengths instead of my challenges. Other students would ask me for help. It felt incredible to be noticed and to give help instead of being the one getting help. It was a gift to support others and to be a role model.

Beginning the program in January meant my class would take an extra semester of courses over the summer to catch up with the September entry group and graduate simultaneously with them the following June. So once again, I was hard at work in school for eighteen solid months. I appreciated the quiet in the building and the extra closeness I had with my classmates. I was enjoying the courses, despite feeling like they were being quite the grind.

Was I ever going to finish school?

It became quite obvious that I had a natural talent for accounting. My instructors strongly encouraged me to continue with the professional accounting program. This would mean at least three more years of education. I remember thinking, "They must be kidding. I really don't want to do more schooling." My instructors reassured me that with the professional accountant designation I would have many more options.

Not wanting to let my talent go to waste, I enrolled in the professional accountant program. It was an intense program requiring thirty to forty hours of study per week in addition to full-time employment. My Business Administration Diploma left me short one credit to transfer the first three years of credits for the program. I decided to take the one credit in Information Systems the following summer, so that I could complete the course requirements for the first three years of study.

I then started the next September in Level 4 of the program. At this point, I had been enrolled in classes for twenty solid months with another eight months ahead of me before I could take a break. I was still living with my parents and working very sporadically in summer jobs.

Finally, after several years of what seemed like constant study, I graduated with my professional accounting designation. Taking the Oath of Obligation was one of the proudest moments of my life. Having both my parents there to see it happen was very special. My employer, also a professional accountant, attended my graduation dinner with a member of his staff. He presented me with a beautiful gold desk clock that still sits on my desk today. It's a beautiful reminder of where I've come from and what I've achieved. Mostly, it's a reminder of those who supported me along the way.

One of my employers advised me that, in his experience, it takes ten years longer to get where you want to go than you think it will. Well, it's my experience that this is indeed true. By the time I had completed my schooling, I had ten years of post-secondary education under my belt. I was now ready to enter the world of work full-time.

In life, when you set out on your path you may often find there are detours. You may be sidetracked because you are not on your best path. It may be because time is needed for you or others to shift and get the most out of the opportunity. If it is meant to be, you will be guided once again in the direction of your best interest. You may not always succeed the first time. If you keep focused on your goal and learn from your mistakes, you can move forward with a renewed sense of commitment. Through learning and reflection you will be more likely to succeed.

It has been my experience, success is not defined by achievements but by one's willingness to hold true to what one feels is right, to move forward one step at a time with commitment, action, and perseverance.

The ability to persevere has taught me more than any grade of excellence ever would have. The success earned through perseverance has taught me to manage my time and to work with others. It has given me the chance to discover options and make choices. It has given me a depth of character and experience I otherwise would not possess. It has allowed me the opportunity to be a leader and a role model. It has allowed me the chance to pause and follow the guidance of others. Being there for others as well as allowing them to be there for me provided an opportunity for everyone involved to learn and grow and reach new levels of understanding.

Celebrate the Silver Lining

As you review the exercises below, be mindful of these key treasures:

1. As we move along our path, we may encounter detours. The detour can serve as a time of evaluation and growth When the time is right, you will often find you will be guided in the direction of your best interest.

2. One definition of success is the ability to hold true to what you feel is right for you.

3. Obstacles and challenges often provide an opportunity to be a leader or a role model. They can offer you a chance to guide others and be guided by others. These interactions can provide a catalyst of greater understanding of yourself, others, and situations.

Take note of what comes to mind as you consider the following in your own life.

1. Think of a time when you had a plan or a goal and there seemed to be a detour or a block to getting what you wanted. Did you eventually get back on track to your original goal? If not, do you

feel that was for the best? What did the detours teach you?

2. How do you personally define success? Think of examples of people who also likely define success this way? Do you use your personal definition of success to guide your decisions?

3. Think of a time when you were called to lead or be a role model. Was the situation simple or was there a challenge involved? Where there times when even as a leader you learned from others? What did the group learn?

Chapter 7 – Where Is My Next Gig?

"Let go or be dragged."

—Zen Proverb

Freedom. Independence. Self-reliance. Choice. This is what a happy, healthy life is made of in my opinion. I believe to attain these things you must first have your health. After that, the key is to have money. To have money, you need a job or another source of financial flow. You need financial resources to meet your financial obligations and experience what you want out of life.

I was taught to get an education and then get a steady job. This was supposedly the key to a successful life. My experience has been life doesn't always work out the way you think it will, despite your best efforts.

Most of my friends started working in high school. They would wait tables, work in retail, or have some other labor-based job. These types of jobs weren't an option for me because I was unable to use my hands and be mobile at the same time. I needed a desk job. For that I needed an education.

In high school while my peers were working, I didn't have a job. I saved the money I was given for birthdays and Christmases because I didn't know when I would need it. Then I graduated high school and started university. Most summers, I had a job, yet even then, there were times when summers went by and I didn't find employment.

I had everything I needed at home with Mom and Dad. Yet not earning my own income led me to feel I was missing out on something. I was seeking a sense of contributing, a sense of autonomy, and a sense of being in the flow of life.

My first full-time job was as an accounting clerk for a transportation company. I worked there for about two years for little more than minimum wage.

As I was already in the fourth level of a professional accounting program, I felt like I deserved much more. However, as I was a student with limited experience, I took what I could get. The hours were long. The job was demanding and I was often faced with challenging dynamics. I was studying thirty to forty hours a week and working another forty hours a week.

Two months after taking my next accounting exam, I found out I didn't pass the course. This was devastating. I was putting all this energy into a job, being overlooked for promotions, and on top of it I didn't pass my course. I had reached my limit—I quit! I gave two weeks' notice and left my job.

Thankfully, I was still living at home with Mom and Dad so I wasn't worried about finances.

It took me nine months before I would find my next job. The salary was much more in line with what my skills warranted. The people were supportive and I learned a great deal. I felt like I made a difference. They had hired me under a one-year contract. I worked as hard as I could and did my best. My contract was extended a few months and eventually they offered me a permanent job. A real full-time permanent job with a solid salary!

I had a job with nice people I was comfortable working with. I was making a difference in the world. I was happy.

With that, I had now worked for them for a year and a half. My graduation from accounting was on the horizon. It was finally time for me to move out on my own.

I had saved a fair amount of money and was able to buy a condo. The woman I purchased the condo from was a schoolteacher; she wanted to keep her condo until June before moving out. That was six months after the date we signed the contract for me to purchase the unit. June seemed so far away. I waited anxiously until moving day finally arrived. At last, I had a place of my own.

Everything was going well. Then about six months later, I was given a layoff notice from the job I loved. They told me I was one of the best employees they had and that if it was simply a matter of poor performance, they would pick someone else to let go. However, my job was nonessential and the company needed to make cutbacks, so I was the one to go.

They gave me a glowing reference, a wonderful farewell, and three months' working notice. Three months came and went and I still had no job.

I was worried about how things would all come together. I would qualify for employment insurance and yet I knew that money wouldn't last forever. I had waited for everything to be just perfect before I moved out. Then, through no fault of my own, I lost my job. I did everything right. I was doing a great job. I was well-liked and yet I was not secure.

I was unemployed for six months. Fortunately, I was good at managing money and I was able to stretch my employment insurance to cover all my expenses. I still worried though.

Then one day, another wonderful opportunity appeared. I was offered a position as an accounting clerk at a major accounting firm. It was quite the opportunity. It was well-paying and, being with such a good company, it would give me great experience. It was for maternity leave coverage for one year.

I loved the job and I mastered it quickly. I loved the people and being part of a bigger company. They appreciated me and told me my job could be permanent if I wanted it. The woman I was replacing was scheduled to come back. They were going to find a place for both of us.

At this point, however, I decided I wanted a change; I would go elsewhere. I had wanted to move to Vancouver for a while. This would be my opportunity to relocate.

Working in the accounting office of the same company in its Vancouver branch was quite different. People had different expectations and communicated differently. I was transferred to three different departments until about a year later they laid me off. I just hadn't found my place there.

Once again, I survived on employment insurance until my next job.

My expenses were higher in Vancouver than in Winnipeg and yet this time I was less worried about making ends meet. I had learned from prior experience that worrying doesn't help. I had confidence that somehow things would work out and I would be fine.

A few months later, I found a job as an accounting manager for a local property development consultant. Once again, the job was a maternity leave position for a year. I did well and was well-liked. Later, it was discovered that the woman I was replacing had decided not to return to work. The job was mine full-time, permanent. Or so it seemed.

I am known for being passionate about making continuous improvement both personally and in business systems. I had implemented many improvements in the small office. As a result, I went from a job that I struggled to manage in an eight-hour day to a job that took half a day to complete. The writing was once again on the wall. In January 2009, I was given a glowing performance review and was told my position was being reduced to half-time. The efficiencies I implemented had worked me out of a job. My team encouraged me to stay. Despite how much I enjoyed it there, I declined their offer. I felt I had outgrown the position and I was looking for something with more responsibility and challenge.

This time, I found a new opportunity quickly. In March I was offered a job as an accounting manager for a service company. I did well there. I made many improvements, learned a great deal, and worked very hard for many years. In fact, it was the first of seven jobs where I was able to stay for longer than two years. I actually worked there eight years. They were like family to me.

But once again my time was coming to an end. Due to a restructuring of the company, I was given a choice to remain in my position or take a layoff. Understanding what that meant for the company long-term, and wanting to do what was best for everyone involved, I accepted the layoff. This was my sixth layoff notice.

There is a consistent lesson across my layoffs. When the writing is on the wall, read the words carefully and let go. Unemployment is an opportunity. Something better always comes along. There may be a wait. The break can be a blessing. Use your time wisely. Eventually there will be space made for you where appropriate.

I have always been provided for, whether it be through employment insurance, employer support, or savings. I've always been able to make ends meet.

Worrying about the future is pointless. It's important to have a backup plan because you never know when your plans are going to take a turn. At the same time, do not waste time waiting for the perfect opportunity before you move forward in life. If something is important to you, do your due diligence, plan carefully, and then make your move.

What is important is you live your life. Do what is right for you even when the outcome is uncertain. Have faith in your own abilities. Do not stay somewhere you know you have outgrown because you are scared to leave or afraid of the unknown. It is important to trust your instincts and look at the big picture.

Celebrate the Silver Lining

As you review the exercises below consider these key treasures:

1. View an ending as an opportunity. The new is almost always greater than the old. Also remember a break from the routine can be a blessing.

2. Worrying about the future does not serve in moving you forward. Plan well and then make your move. Waiting for your idea of perfection may cost you in the long run.

3. Do what you believe is right even if the outcome is uncertain. Have faith in your abilities and trust your instincts.

Take note of what comes to mind as you consider the following:

1. Think of a time when things had an unexpected ending that eventually led to something even better. How did you initially react when your plans did not work out? Reflecting on this situation, how are you likely to react in the future when faced with an ending?

2. When faced with making a change, have you ever waited for perfection before moving forward? Was the wait worth it? What did it cost you?

3. Have you ever moved forward quickly without considering pitfalls? Was it worth the risk? What did moving forward quickly cost you?

4. Make a list of your strengths. How can these help you when faced with uncertainty?

Chapter 8 – What's My Next Move?

"Dare to live the life you've always wanted."

—Anonymous

Home is truly where the heart is. As mentioned earlier, in October 2005, I moved from Winnipeg to Vancouver. I wanted a more challenging job and getting a transfer with my accounting firm seemed like a good opportunity to relocate to Vancouver. I'd always felt an attraction to the city. I liked the energy and the vibrancy there. I knew the city was more densely populated and there was more activity at night. This made the streets feel safer.

When I first thought of making the move, I wondered if the city would still hold the same attraction as it had those years ago when I was training for track and field with the national coach. A friend of mine suggested I plan a trip there and see if I still felt drawn to Vancouver.

I took her advice and for Christmas vacation 2004 I spent a week in Vancouver. I learned some basics about the city's layout, became familiar with public transit, and visited some attractions. I continually reflected on how I felt about being there and I went about my day as if I lived there. I returned from my vacation with the knowledge that Vancouver still held my interest as it had ten years earlier. But I wasn't yet convinced that I wanted to move there.

There was to be a conference the following spring when all my company's financial advisory divisions across Canada came together. It was to be in Niagara Falls, Ontario. Once there, I did some networking with the Vancouver manager; I was bored with my life in Winnipeg. I wanted a different lifestyle. I also wanted to live in a city with more convenient public transportation. I was in a rut.

I sat with the decision to move or not to move for about six months after that. The move seemed daunting and having to give up everything I'd ever known for something unknown was very scary.

Finally, I decided I would pack up and go.

The deciding factor was, if I didn't like it, I could always come back. However, if I didn't go I would never know what could have been. I didn't want to live the rest of my life wondering what could have happened.

In August, I booked a seven-day cruise to Alaska. I arrived in Vancouver three days before I was scheduled to set sail. I had prearranged to spend those days interviewing for a transfer with my accounting firm and buying a condo. That is exactly what happened. The Vancouver office hired me on the spot.

The housing market in Vancouver moves very fast. It is common for properties to sell in a couple of days. I viewed the place one day and bought it two days later.

I remember rushing to sign the offer on my condo and then immediately heading to the cruise dock in downtown

Vancouver. I enjoyed sharing my adventures of the past few days with fellow passengers. I had a wonderful time on my cruise. The scenery was breathtaking, the excursions were amazing, and the boat was spectacular. It was the perfect end to celebrate my decision to start a new life.

Shortly after I returned home from my vacation in Alaska, I took my parents for a nice dinner and told them of my decision. To say they were shocked is an understatement. It was hard for them to understand why I would want to give up being close to family. To them every city was essentially the same; it was family that mattered.

Regardless of how they felt about the situation, as always, they gave me their full support. With that, two months later on Thanksgiving weekend October 2005, I boarded my first train ever and journeyed west to my new home in the beautiful City of Vancouver.

I quickly discovered I love trains. I love the nostalgia, the simplicity, the freedom, the sounds, and the motion. It all felt refreshingly natural in a world made up of rules and regulations. The journey by train was lovely, uneventful really.

Then all of a sudden without warning, ka-thud, my train derailed! We were ten minutes from the station in Vancouver. So close and yet so far. We waited there for half an hour until the crew came and righted the train back on its tracks. It was a minor inconvenience resulting in a delay, nothing serious. It was a reminder that things can change quickly, when least expected, and that things don't always work out as planned. The derailment would be a metaphor for things to come.

There were parts of adjusting to my new life in Vancouver that were easy. There were parts that were more difficult than I expected. In fact, I remember all the things I thought would be easy were actually quite difficult, while the things I had expected to be difficult were much easier. I think I evaluated the level of challenge relative to what I expected.

As I began to settle into my condo, I felt quite isolated when I discovered I didn't have a phone book and I had not yet had the Internet installed. I also didn't yet have my cell phone. Being new to the city and not knowing where anything was located or how to access anything made things quite challenging.

I quickly learned there is no Walmart in downtown Vancouver. It is a densely populated city and the land is used mostly for housing. The stores are smaller and closer together. Big box stores are found in the surrounding areas outside Vancouver. Walmart had been my go-to for basic shopping for years. I now had to find somewhere new for the everyday basics. In fact, the last straw was when I wanted to buy socks and learned there was no Walmart. I had absolutely no idea where to go and I didn't know anyone who could tell me the answer. A simple thing like socks threw me over the edge.

One day an amazing thing happened. I was shopping. In my rush to leave one store, I left my wallet behind at a checkout stand When I arrived home and realized my wallet was missing, my first thought was, "My only hope is if an honest accountant finds it."

Well, as luck would have it, that's exactly what happened. I had a slip of paper in my wallet from a taxi company linking me to that company and my accounting firm. In a couple of days, I received a call—my wallet had been found. The next day I made arrangements to meet the woman who had found it.

My transition to Vancouver continued to be bumpy. But having my wallet returned restored my faith that things would be alright.

As I mentioned, I stayed at my job at the accounting firm for about a year. It didn't work out as planned. I was transferred to three different departments while I was there. There were often times when people disappointed me. Things were different than they first appeared to be. This was life in the big city. Eventually I moved to a new job and felt I had found a meaningful place in the world.

As I remember, it took about a year and a half for me to fully adjust to life in Vancouver. In some ways, my new city instantly felt like home. I loved what it had to offer. It was filled with many new and exciting opportunities.

In other ways, my journey was met with disappointment and adversity. There was a period of time when I considered moving back to Winnipeg. I knew everything I experienced was for learning and growth and served as a reflection of how I viewed the world. I reminded myself of why I originally moved to Vancouver. I also remained connected to my heart's desire to expand and explore.

In the end, that desire helped push me through any challenge. I emerged stronger, wiser, and more capable than ever to rise to the next challenge. I have now lived in Vancouver for over ten years. I am profoundly grateful for daring to venture into the unknown. I know I have had many different opportunities and experiences because of it. My choice required many sacrifices. I am indeed much richer for it.

Celebrate the Silver Lining

To help you review this chapter, here are some key treasures:

1. If you are moving forward and the going gets tough, stay focused on the reasons why you chose to pursue your goal. This and staying connected to your heart's desire can serve as very powerful tools to move you through challenges.

2. Sometimes when working to achieve your goals, you may be faced with disappointment or be required to make sacrifices. Accepting this is key.

3. When we follow our heart and commit to the goal despite the required sacrifices, the rewards of success often more than make up for the difficulties along the way.

Take note of what comes to you as you consider the following in your own life:

1. Write down a goal that you are currently working toward. List all

the reasons why it is important to you. Mark which reasons are the most important to you. Pick one or two reasons. Let these main reasons be a source of strength for you as you move toward your goal.

2. What have you sacrificed or let go of that has helped you get to where you are with your goal? What might you still need to let go of to help you reach your goal?

3. Write down a goal that you have already achieved. Make note of some of the challenges you met along the way. Make note of the rewards. What do you notice?

Chapter 9 – Can You Lend a Hand?

"When we allow ourselves to adapt
to different situations, life is easier."
—*Catherine Pulsifer*

If you're anything like me, you've wondered "What if ...?" Using walking supports all my life, I would often notice others who would be using walking aids due to injury and wonder, "What if I were injured? How would I get around? I'm already using canes." Well, one day I had my answer.

I was sitting at the computer, searching the Internet one night, when I reached down to pick something off the floor and was thrown off balance. I was part way out of the chair. I was faced with the choice to pull myself up or let myself fall. Normally, letting myself fall is the easiest and safest option. My life experience to this point had been "Don't fight gravity." So with that in mind, I chose to fall to the floor.

Now there was one factor I had not considered when making my choice. My desk area was a relatively small space. When I fell to the ground, there was not enough space for my hands to fully stretch out and absorb the fall.

Snap! Bones actually do make a noise when they break. The pain in my hand was excruciating. I felt dizzy and nauseous as I lay on the floor until my body settled itself. I sat up and realized I would need medical attention. It was almost ten o'clock on a Saturday night. The emergency room would be jammed. It was highly likely it would be the early hours of the morning before I would see a doctor. With that in mind, I decided to head off to bed and deal with the situation in the morning after a good night's sleep.

I slept fairly well, even though, when I moved in my sleep, I would press on my injured hand and be abruptly awakened by sharp rushes of pain.

Eventually morning arrived. I decided I was feeling better and before going off to the hospital I ventured to my spiritual center where I spent most Sunday mornings. The ninety-minute journey on transit was alright as long as I avoided pressing on my hand.

At the center, I met several friends and showed them what I had accomplished the night before. By the time I arrived at the center, my hand was quite swollen. After the service, my friend—let's call her Leah—said she would take me to the hospital. I was so happy to have help. I appreciated having a ride back to the hospital close to home ninety-minutes away. To have someone wait with me the long hours before I saw the doctor helped the time pass quickly.

There was more waiting to get an x-ray after seeing the doctor. Then of course more waiting for the results of the x-ray. I was grateful to have Leah's support, companionship, and conversation. The x-rays confirmed that a bone in my left hand was indeed broken. Specifically, I had broken a bone in my ring finger.

Thank goodness the break was in my left hand. I would have been rendered useless if it had been my right hand. I am right-handed and in no way ambidextrous. Always be thankful for small blessings.

With the x-ray results, the doctor proceeded to set my hand and cast it. I remember being amazed at how gentle the process was. The doctor froze my hand and then very gently proceeded to slowly realign my ring finger with its neighbors. Then he began to wrap plaster in a half cast around my hand and up my arm. A tensor bandage completed the job, holding the cast on my arm.

I was asked to wait for a second set of x-rays. I was told my type of fracture is often very unstable, and surgery might be necessary. Leah and I went for dinner at the hospital cafeteria. The food was surprisingly quite good. It was a long day and I was hungry. I enjoyed our conversation. After dinner, I proceeded to get my second set of x-rays, which revealed good news. My fracture was set and stable. Surgery avoided. Another blessing.

Now the question was "How am I going to walk out of here with a cast on my arm? I will be unable to grip my canes." I knew there must be a way. I was interested to see just what this would look like. A nurse returned with a walker with wheels. At the side where hands normally grip was a rest to cradle my arm. My arm was to be held in place with Velcro straps.

Having an arm in a cast was not the hardest part. The hardest part was that the walker they gave me didn't steer very well. The wheels didn't move properly and it was incredibly hard to turn and manipulate. "One step at a time," I thought. "This too shall pass."

With my new walking aid in tow, I was set to go home. As I fumbled to get in the car, I was so happy to have my friend Leah with me. I had not thought about how I could possibly handle a walker and canes *and* a broken hand. Once I was at home, my friend Leah made sure I was safely in my condo. She then helped me take my garbage out and finally said goodnight.

That night, I had difficulty sleeping. Despite elevating my arm on a pillow as the doctor directed, my hand ached and throbbed. When I woke the next morning for work, I started to realize just how different things would be for the next three weeks until my hand healed. I was very grateful it would only be three weeks. My previous experiences with casts involved six to eight weeks.

As I've said, I usually walk around the house unaided. The weight of the cast on my arm threw me off balance if I walked without support. I would need the walker for everything now, even for a few steps. Having a walker with me everywhere I went and for every step I took was a major inconvenience. Thankfully, I was able to shower with a plastic bag on my hand. I viewed this as a relatively minor inconvenience.

Getting dressed, however, proved to be extra challenging. Doing up zippers, fastening buttons, and making sure sleeves were over my cast required new skills that would take a few days to master. Everything took so much longer. I was so thankful to be working remotely from home. That would save me the time and hassle of commuting on transit.

My coworkers were very helpful. Any documents that needed to be signed or reviewed were brought to my home. I could quickly review them and they would be taken back to the office the next day. My phone was ringing off the hook. The current focus of my job not only involved the usual supervising of the monthly tasks but also the coordination of an office renovation and an eventual move to a new location. There were so many calls to make. I had a constant stream of emails and questions from every direction. There was no rest for me. I couldn't skip a beat.

Two days later, I finally had time to catch my breath. As my workday ended, I shut down my computer and flopped down on the chair in my living room. I let out a deep sigh of exhaustion. I then proceeded to beat the upholstery of the chair in frustration. I had been on the go nonstop since Sunday at the hospital. This was the first moment I could really be with the experience of my broken hand.

"Why did I choose to fall? I didn't have to do that. If things were placed to allow for more spaciousness in this room, it wouldn't have happened," I thought. "Saturday night I was tired. Why was I looking up stuff on the Internet anyway?"

I don't remember what it was. It all seemed like such a waste.

To top it all off, in two days was the start of a four-day cultural festival. I was volunteering with the events and at one of the booths. What a drag to be laid up right before the festival. Well, I wasn't going to let it stop me. I wanted to keep my commitments and, what's even more, I wanted to be at the festival. Plain and simple, I was definitely going to go despite the state of my hand.

While I was resting and contemplating why I had made my choice to fall, I knew on some level the situation was the teach me something.

The next day I decided to stop acting sick. Time to move on. I tidied up the house. I began to figure out how I would get out of my apartment. I had a heavy door to maneuver and a walker that wouldn't steer well. In time, I realized if I placed the walker in a certain spot I could open the door, move forward, and place my walker in the doorway, then keep moving forward until I was out of the house with the door closed behind me.

Okay, great! Next task. It was a short walk down the hall to the elevator. I stood at the elevator and pressed the call button. When it arrived, I awkwardly maneuvered my walker into the elevator and scanned my fob to go downstairs. This was relatively easy. My third task was getting out of the front door of my apartment building. There was a button to push beside the door to unlock it. Then, I still had to open the door manually and walk through. Similarly to what I had learned in my apartment, I learned there was a certain way I could put my walker as I held the door and walked through. I did it! I was outside. I was no longer confined to my apartment. What an amazing feeling.

I stayed outside for a while and enjoyed the fresh air before returning back into my condo. "Wait! How am I getting back into my apartment?" I thought I had to scan the fob next to the intercom, which was a few feet away from the door. This would unlock the front door for thirty seconds. Then I had to hold the door open and walk into the lobby. Once again, I would have to master angles and place my walker in just the right spot. My task was to reach the magnetic strip for the entry and quickly move over toward the door before it locked thirty seconds later. I used my walker to hold the door open as I walked through it and closed the door behind me.

Well, it was a challenge. Mission accomplished! My practice was successful. Now, I felt I could leave home.

At the festival, I was able to perform my duties well and with my usual enthusiasm. They mostly involved greeting people and keeping track of inventory and cash sales. People at the festival were inspired that I showed up despite the inconvenience of my injured hand. As I said, for me, not showing up simply wasn't an option. I wanted to be at the festival and, therefore, I made it happen.

During the three weeks with my hand in a cast, I also learned how to manipulate my walker onto the ramp of the bus. I had to find new ways of shopping for a few things, but I waited until my hand was out of the cast before I did any major shopping.

I believe I was given the challenge of experiencing a broken hand for many reasons. I had the opportunity to ask for help from friends and others around me. I realized I had more support in the world than I thought I had. I learned to get outside my routine and find different ways of solving problems. I experienced immense satisfaction as I discovered a deeper knowing of my resourcefulness. Also, I developed a deeper sense of gratitude for the mobility I do have.

Celebrate the Silver Lining

As you review the exercises below, let these key treasures serve as a guide:

1. Obstacles often serve as opportunities to speak up and ask for help. Learning to

communicate in this way can be quite rewarding.

2. Asking for help can draw your attention to the level of support you already have. This may lead to a new understanding of what and who you have around you.

3. Facing challenges offers opportunities to learn new skills and experience satisfaction once you've mastered them. Challenges can also give you a new level of gratitude for all that is going well in your life.

Take note of what comes to mind as you consider the following:

1. Think of a time when asking for help led to an unexpected benefit beyond your initial request.

2. Think of a time when you asked for support. Did you receive more than you expected? Think about what often happens when people are faced with natural disasters.

3. Think of a time when you did something by accident. What did it teach you? Did you gain a new level of satisfaction or gratitude?

Chapter 10 – Is There a Doctor in the House?

"Seeking Clarity is seeking connection with the
universe. To connect is to understand;
to be clear is to be enlightened."
—Annie Zelezsak

Life is made up of moments. In a single moment, life can change from ordinary to extraordinary if you are paying attention. I was recently in Northern California, staffing a retreat. For Sunday breakfast, I was led to sit at the back of the dining hall by the door I don't usually sit there.

My day started like any other morning. I sat down to eat and began a conversation with the woman across from me. I don't remember being careless in any way as I ate my breakfast. One moment I was eating and the next I was choking (on a piece of kiwi fruit, I think). This was beyond anything I had ever experienced. I was really choking. I could breathe ... barely.

I was coughing and nothing was moving. People in the dining hall asked around. No one knew the Heimlich maneuver. The retreat site was at the top of a mountain. I knew the drive up from the main road took thirty minutes. I knew it was up to me. I put the thought out that I needed help. I was thankful to be by the door when this was happening; because anywhere else would have been quite disruptive.

I knew it wasn't my time. I also knew I needed serious help. I began to cough as hard as I could. I thought about this book and the speaking I was planning to do. I thought of the volumes of lessons I have to share with the world. A minute or two later, the majority of what was lodged in my throat had come out.

I still felt a tightness in my chest and would spit up every few minutes. It seemed to ease up with time. However, hours later, I was still unable to walk across the room without being sick. I was also unable to swallow almost anything, even water. My breathing was restored; however, it seemed I had a blockage or a spasm in my esophagus.

I knew I needed to resolve the situation sooner rather than later. I didn't understand what was happening with my body, so I reluctantly went to the hospital. A team member drove me down the mountain to a hospital that was an hour away. My symptoms remained unchanged.

Finally after being seen by the admitting nurse and having my blood pressure taken, whatever blockage I was experiencing released. The tightness of the blood pressure cuff around my arm triggered a movement in my body that shifted things. I felt a profound tightness in my chest as the cuff tightened. Then in an instant I felt as though I had returned to normal.

I stayed to see the doctor and have the recommended x-ray just to be sure everything had indeed restored to normal. I was flying the next day and had to be well. As expected, the x-ray confirmed everything was normal. With that, we began the hour's drive that would eventually wind back up the mountain to the retreat.

We returned to the retreat at what seemed to be the perfect time. I was welcomed back with an energetic round of applause. I received so much love in that moment, and so much love throughout the day with people checking in and showing their concern. I recognized that the incident was somewhat disruptive to the retreat. Yet I didn't feel poorly for any of the help I was given. It was necessary and I didn't feel I was careless in any way to have caused the incident. Sometimes in life, things simply happen.

There are times when we all truly need help. Being able to receive is a wonderful gift. What I received that day was genuine support and connection with others. I knew I had a special place in their hearts. My presence mattered. The blockage in my throat gifted me with a renewed sense of clarity of my place in the world. It breathed new life into my book and fuelled my desire to launch myself into the future, sharing my voice with others. This may just be my greatest gift of all.

Celebrate the Silver Lining

As you review the exercises below, here are some key treasures:

1. Being able to receive fully and without judgment is a wonderful gift. It gives you a sense of appreciation and connection with others that fuels you to embrace life. It also gives others the gift of being able to give to you and it helps them feel a sense of purpose and connection.

2. Adversity, especially when unexpected, can give clarity to your priorities.

3. Adversity can create a sense of urgency in a situation. That sense of urgency can then help us move forward more effectively in other areas of life.

Take note of what comes to you as you consider the following in your own life:

1. Make note of a time when you were able to give something to someone else. How did you feel? Did the act of giving leave you feeling fulfilled?

2. Make note of a time when adversity caused you to shift your priorities. Did the shift have positive results?

3. Make note of a time when adversity helped you move forward on a project that previously lacked urgency. What were the results?

Conclusion

"Be thankful for what you have; you'll end up having more. If you concentrate on what you don't have, you will never, ever have enough."
—Oprah Winfrey

As you move through your life experience, there is no question you will encounter obstacles. Everyone does. Remember how you choose to see them is up to you. If you focus on what you have instead of what you don't have, your path will almost certainly become easier. What's more is if you focus on what you have, you will receive the beautiful gift at the end of the rainbow.

It is important to honor where you are at any given moment. Challenges can bring pain, fear, frustration, and a multitude of other stresses. Acknowledge your feelings. Give yourself time to feel them. That is often the first step in moving through a challenge. The key is to turn your attention to the silver lining or the blessing you are receiving. When you seek to find the blessing, it is there you will find the joy.

There are many blessings to be found inside obstacles. They help strengthen our inner qualities so we develop new and different aspects of ourself. Almost always moving through challenges requires the support of others. By connecting with others, we learn new skills and our relationships grow. Interacting with others offers the opportunity to gain a fresh perspective. Sharing with those who have lived a similar experience can lead to a deeper understanding of ourself and those around us.

Life can be very busy. It is common to get lost in the rush to succeed and lose sight of what is the next best step. Obstacles often provide an opportunity to pause. In the pause is a chance to physically, mentally, and emotionally slow down and rest. It offers a time to go within and re-evaluate what you want or what you feel is right. You may notice you've moved away from your goal and need to make a correction to get back on track. You may also simply realize your heart's desire has shifted and it's time for a new venture. A pause can serve to be a defining moment of profound clarity. It can serve to be the seed of something much greater.

As you journey through life, it's quite possible that even the best-made plans don't evolve as intended. It's important to bring with you a plan B and a safety net. This will help you let go of fear and the need for perfection before moving forward. Learn to love the unknown and expect the unexpected. Live your life to the best of your ability. Embrace the world around you. All anyone has is a series of moments. By embracing a new opportunity and the challenges it often brings, you will find you have a much greater sense of gratitude and joy in your life. As you let the light shine in your life, you become a role model and a source of inspiration for others. The ripple effect has infinite possibilities for everyone.

Review Request

What did you think of this short book? Was it helpful to you? I'd be so grateful if you'd leave a short review on Amazon.

You can connect with Kathryn:

and get your bonus gifts at:

inspiredbykathryn.com

joyofobstacles.com

Made in the USA
Columbia, SC
09 November 2018